"The Secret Formula to Winning YouTube Sponsorships"

Introduction

In today's digital age, YouTube has become a powerhouse platform, offering immense opportunities for content creators to build a personal brand, engage with audiences, and generate income. One of the most lucrative ways to monetise your channel is through sponsorships, but securing the right partnerships can often feel like a daunting task.

This ebook, *The Secret to YouTube Sponsorship Success*, is designed to guide you through the process of attracting, negotiating, and maintaining successful sponsorships. Whether you're just starting out or looking to elevate your existing channel, this comprehensive guide provides proven strategies, practical tips, and insider insights into the world of YouTube sponsorships.

We'll explore everything from identifying the right sponsors for your niche, to crafting compelling proposals and building long-term, mutually beneficial relationships. You'll learn how to present yourself as an attractive partner to brands and how to maximise the financial rewards without compromising your authenticity or audience trust.

With the right approach, YouTube sponsorships can open doors to not just financial success, but to exciting collaborations and partnerships that fuel your growth. Let's unlock the secrets to YouTube sponsorship success together and take your channel to new heights.

Index

1. **Define Your Niche:** Be clear on the specific audience you serve, as brands look for creators with targeted followings that match their products.

2. **Build a Strong Personal Brand:** Establish a unique identity that resonates with viewers and brands alike, showing what sets you apart from others.

3. **Create High-Quality Content:** Consistently upload well-produced, engaging content that will attract both viewers and potential sponsors.

4. **Engage with Your Audience:** Foster a loyal community through interactions, responding to comments, and creating content based on their interests.

5. **Reach a Solid Subscriber Count:** While large numbers aren't everything, a solid, engaged audience is crucial to attracting the right sponsors.

6. **Have a Professional Media Kit:** A well-designed media kit showcasing your statistics, audience demographics, and past brand collaborations can make a powerful impression.

7. **Understand Your Analytics:** Use YouTube's analytics to demonstrate your reach, viewer demographics, and engagement rates to potential sponsors.

8. **Showcase Your Value Proposition:** Brands want to know how working with you will benefit them. Be clear about the value you bring.

9. **Reach Out to Brands:** Don't wait for brands to come to you. Proactively reach out with a pitch tailored to their needs and values.

10. **Negotiate Fairly:** Ensure that you are compensated fairly for your work, keeping in mind both your time and the exposure you're providing the brand.

11. **Build Long-Term Relationships:** Rather than one-off deals, aim to establish lasting partnerships with brands that align with your values.

12. **Stay Authentic:** Only work with brands that align with your channel's ethos and audience interests to maintain trust and authenticity.

13. **Create Sponsored Content Naturally:** Seamlessly integrate sponsored content into your videos, making sure it aligns with your regular content style.

14. **Offer Exclusive Deals or Discounts:** Provide value to your audience with special deals or discount codes from your sponsors, further enhancing the partnership.

15. **Follow Legal and Ethical Guidelines:** Ensure you follow all advertising regulations, such as clear disclosures and honest reviews, to maintain transparency and trust with your audience.

Chapter-01

Define Your Niche: Be clear on the specific audience you serve, as brands look for creators with targeted followings that match their products.

In the vast and dynamic world of YouTube, the term "niche" refers to the specific segment of the platform that a creator focuses on. It's the unique space that defines what content you produce, who your audience is, and the specific topics, interests, or themes you cover. Whether it's beauty tutorials, tech reviews, cooking recipes, or educational content, defining your niche is a crucial step in positioning yourself as a creator of value. This step not only helps you stand out in a crowded market but also plays a key role in securing sponsorships from brands that align with your content and audience.

The Importance of Defining Your Niche

YouTube is home to millions of creators, each offering a variety of content across a range of categories. In this sea of creators, being clear about your niche allows you to carve out a space for yourself. It makes it easier for viewers to find and connect with your content, and more importantly, it makes it easier for brands to identify you as a potential partner. Sponsorships are driven by the ability of a creator to reach a specific target audience, and brands are always looking for creators whose audience aligns with their products or services.

When you define your niche, you set yourself up to attract sponsorships from brands that are seeking to reach a very specific consumer group. For instance, a creator in the fitness niche will appeal to brands selling health supplements, gym equipment, or activewear. Similarly, a beauty influencer with a focus on cruelty-free makeup will attract brands that prioritise ethical, sustainable products.

By narrowing your focus and appealing to a specific audience, you are not just attracting any sponsor, but those who are genuinely interested in your niche and are willing to invest in it. This can result in more authentic, long-term partnerships that are both profitable and mutually beneficial.

How to Define Your Niche

Identify Your Passion and Expertise

The first step in defining your niche is to identify what you are passionate about and where your expertise lies. What topics excite you, and what can you talk about endlessly? Whether it's gaming, fashion, education, or cooking, your niche should reflect both your interests and knowledge. This ensures that your content is authentic, engaging, and sustainable in the long term.

Understand Your Audience

Once you've identified your passion, consider the type of audience that would be interested in it. Who are the people you want to engage with? What are their interests, demographics, and needs? By understanding your audience, you can better tailor your content to meet their expectations, and this will help you attract the right sponsorships.

Research the Competition

Look at other creators in your space. What are they doing, and how can you differentiate yourself? Researching your competition gives you an understanding of the existing market and allows you to position yourself uniquely. You can identify gaps or underserved areas within your niche that you can capitalise on.

Narrow Down Your Focus

The more specific you can be with your niche, the more appealing you will be to potential sponsors. While it may seem counterintuitive, narrowing your focus helps you stand out. For example, instead of just focusing on "fitness," you could focus on "home workout routines for busy professionals" or "fitness for seniors." This specificity makes you more attractive to sponsors looking to target those specific demographics.

Test and Refine Your Niche

Once you've defined your niche, it's important to create content and gauge audience response. Are people engaging with your content? Are brands starting to take notice? If your niche isn't resonating with your target audience or attracting the right kind of sponsorships, be open to refining your focus. It's essential to remain flexible and adaptable as your channel grows.

Benefits of a Defined Niche

Attracting the Right Sponsors

Brands are more likely to reach out to creators whose content aligns with their products. When you have a well-defined niche, you appeal directly to companies looking for an audience that mirrors their target market. A tech brand, for example, will prefer to work with a creator who reviews gadgets or tech products rather than someone whose content focuses on lifestyle topics.

Building an Engaged Community

Having a specific niche allows you to build a dedicated community around your content. When your audience knows what to expect from your channel, they are more likely to return and become engaged viewers. This level of engagement makes your channel more attractive to sponsors, as they want to see proof that you can drive actions and influence your audience's purchasing decisions.

Increased Brand Loyalty

By focusing on a specific niche, you create a sense of loyalty within your audience. They follow you not just for your content, but because you represent a particular interest or lifestyle they are passionate about. This can lead to stronger relationships with your audience and greater success with sponsored content, as loyal viewers are more likely to trust your recommendations.

More Targeted Content Opportunities

When your niche is clear, you can create content that resonates more deeply with your audience, making your channel more attractive to sponsors. Whether it's a product review, a tutorial, or a sponsored challenge, brands are more likely to trust creators who know exactly what their audience values and are able to create content that aligns with those interests.

Higher Conversion Rates

Sponsors are ultimately interested in driving sales or increasing brand awareness. A creator with a clearly defined niche has a higher chance of producing content that converts, meaning viewers are more likely to purchase products or services recommended by the creator. This is a compelling argument for sponsors to partner with you, as they see the potential for a good return on investment.

Conclusion

Defining your niche on YouTube is not just about carving out a specific space for your content, but about positioning yourself as an attractive and valuable partner for potential sponsors. By focusing on a particular audience and providing targeted, consistent content, you create opportunities for long-term growth and success. A well-defined niche helps you attract sponsors who share your values and are looking to reach your specific audience, leading to more authentic partnerships and greater financial rewards. If you haven't already defined your niche, now is the time to start thinking about the type of content you want to create, the audience you want to engage, and the brands that could benefit from a partnership with you. The clearer you are about your niche, the more likely you are to achieve YouTube sponsorship success.

Chapter-02

Build a Strong Personal Brand: Establish a unique identity that resonates with viewers and brands alike, showing what sets you apart from others.

In the highly competitive world of YouTube, creators need more than just good content to stand out. A strong personal brand is crucial for differentiating yourself, resonating with your audience, and attracting opportunities, including sponsorships. A personal brand goes beyond the videos you create; it encompasses your personality, values, style, and how you present yourself to the world. Establishing a unique and recognisable brand identity is a key component of long-term success on YouTube, enabling you to build a dedicated community, connect with like-minded brands, and stand out in a crowded digital landscape.

The Importance of a Strong Personal Brand

A strong personal brand is essential for gaining credibility and trust with both your audience and potential sponsors. With millions of creators on YouTube, having a clear, authentic brand identity helps you differentiate yourself from others. When viewers feel a connection to your personal brand, they are more likely to subscribe, engage with your content, and return regularly. For brands, a creator's personal brand provides assurance that their products or services will be represented in a way that aligns with their values and appeals to their target market.

Building a personal brand isn't just about what you create but about how you present yourself, the message you convey, and the emotions you evoke. A consistent, well-crafted personal brand makes it easier for sponsors to see the potential for collaboration and ensures that any partnership feels authentic. Whether you're a lifestyle vlogger, tech reviewer, or fitness expert, a strong personal brand establishes your credibility, builds trust, and creates a lasting impression on your viewers and brands alike.

How to Build a Strong Personal Brand

Define Your Values and Mission

The first step in building a strong personal brand is to define what you stand for. This means identifying your core values and mission as a creator. What drives you? What do you want to share with the world? Your values should be at the heart of everything you do on YouTube. Whether it's promoting sustainability, mental health awareness, or simply creating educational content, being clear on your mission gives your brand a sense of purpose. When your audience understands your values, they are more likely to connect with your content on a deeper level.

Find Your Unique Voice and Style

To build a personal brand that stands out, you need to develop a unique voice and style. This includes everything from the tone of your videos to the visual elements that make up your channel. Are you casual and humorous, or serious and informative? Your personality should shine through in your content, helping you forge a personal connection with your audience. Similarly, your visual style, including your logo, colours, and thumbnails, should be consistent across all your videos and social media profiles, creating a cohesive and recognisable brand.

Know Your Audience

A strong personal brand is rooted in understanding your audience. You need to know who you're speaking to, what their interests are, and what challenges they face. Knowing your audience allows you to tailor your content to their needs and desires. This helps build a loyal community of viewers who feel like you're speaking directly to them. When brands see that you have a highly engaged and well-defined audience, they are more likely to approach you for sponsorships. The more aligned your audience is with a brand's target market, the more likely they are to want to work with you.

Consistency Is Key

Consistency is one of the most important aspects of building a strong personal brand. You need to be consistent not just in the type of content you create, but also in your posting schedule, tone, and visual identity. Whether you upload once a week or twice a month, being reliable builds trust with your audience and makes you more appealing to brands. When a brand sees that you consistently produce high-quality content that resonates with your audience, they will be more likely to see you as a long-term partner.

Engage and Build Relationships with Your Community

Engagement is a vital part of building your personal brand on YouTube. Responding to comments, interacting on social media, and engaging with your audience during live streams all help strengthen your relationship with them. When your audience feels like they know you and have a personal connection with you, they are more likely to support your content, recommend your channel, and trust your sponsored endorsements. Moreover, creating a community where viewers feel seen and heard can lead to more dedicated followers and more meaningful sponsorship opportunities.

Leverage Social Media to Strengthen Your Brand

Your personal brand extends beyond YouTube, and using other social media platforms to reinforce your identity is essential. Instagram, Twitter, TikTok, and other platforms allow you to interact with your audience in new and diverse ways. Sharing behind-the-scenes content, personal stories, and updates on social media can help humanise your brand and deepen the connection with your followers. These platforms also give you the opportunity to reach new audiences and showcase your content in a different format, which can amplify your personal brand across various online spaces.

Be Authentic and Transparent

One of the key factors in building a strong personal brand is authenticity. Viewers can spot inauthenticity from a mile away, and it can quickly damage your reputation. To create a brand that resonates with others, be true to yourself and let your genuine personality shine. Whether you're promoting a product or sharing a personal story, your audience will appreciate your honesty and transparency. Being authentic not only helps build trust with your audience but also makes you a more attractive partner for brands looking for creators who represent their values with integrity.

The Role of a Personal Brand in Sponsorship Success

A well-established personal brand makes it easier to secure sponsorships because brands want to partner with creators who align with their identity and target audience. When a creator has a strong personal brand, they are more likely to attract brands that share similar values and goals. Additionally, a recognisable personal brand increases your credibility and makes you appear more professional, which is important when negotiating sponsorship deals. Brands are more inclined to invest in creators who consistently deliver high-quality content that aligns with their messaging and values.

Conclusion

Building a strong personal brand on YouTube is essential for long-term success, especially when it comes to attracting sponsorships. By defining your values, establishing a unique voice, and understanding your audience, you can create a brand that resonates with viewers and brands alike. Consistency, engagement, and authenticity are all key components in strengthening your personal brand. When done right, your personal brand becomes not only a reflection of who you are but also a valuable asset that opens doors to exciting opportunities and long-term collaborations with brands.

Chapter-03

Create High-Quality Content: Consistently upload well-produced, engaging content that will attract both viewers and potential sponsors.

In the competitive world of YouTube, creating high-quality content is the cornerstone of any successful channel. It's not just about producing visually appealing videos; high-quality content encompasses everything from the production values and storytelling to the engagement it generates and the value it provides to your audience. Consistently uploading well-produced and engaging videos is essential for building an audience, maintaining viewer interest, and attracting potential sponsors. When done right, high-quality content serves as a powerful tool for brand growth and long-term success on YouTube.

The Importance of High-Quality Content

High-quality content is essential for attracting viewers and sponsors alike. On YouTube, where millions of videos are uploaded daily, it's easy for creators to get lost in the noise. A channel that consistently produces engaging, well-edited content stands out from the crowd and builds a loyal following. When your content is of high quality, your viewers are more likely to return, share your videos, and engage with your brand. Moreover, potential sponsors are always on the lookout for creators who can produce content that will reflect well on their brand and attract their target market.

A channel that consistently produces high-quality content not only gains trust and respect from its audience but also increases the likelihood of long-term partnerships with brands. Companies are more inclined to collaborate with creators who can produce professional, engaging content that aligns with their products or services. By focusing on quality, you make your channel more appealing to sponsors, increasing your chances of securing lucrative deals.

Key Elements of High-Quality Content

Compelling Storytelling

Good content is not just about high-definition visuals and fancy editing; it's also about telling a story. Whether you're reviewing a product, teaching a skill, or vlogging about your daily life, your ability to weave a compelling narrative keeps your viewers engaged. The best creators know how to captivate their audience from the very first few seconds of their video and maintain that interest throughout. A well-crafted story ensures that viewers not only watch your videos but also share them and return for more. Storytelling should evoke emotions, provide value, or solve a problem for your audience, making them feel connected to your content.

Professional Production Quality

Production quality plays a significant role in how your content is perceived. While it's not necessary to have the most expensive equipment, ensuring your videos have clear audio, good lighting, and sharp visuals is crucial. Viewers are more likely to engage with content that is easy to watch and listen to. Basic equipment such as a high-quality microphone, good camera, and proper lighting can make a huge difference in the overall look and feel of your videos. Additionally, editing plays a significant part in maintaining a smooth flow and removing any distractions that may detract from the viewer's experience.

Investing time in editing, ensuring good pacing, and adding relevant graphics or animations can help keep your audience's attention. Properly edited videos with a clear structure and seamless transitions will make your content feel more polished and professional. This enhances the viewing experience and signals to potential sponsors that you take your content creation seriously.

Engagement and Interaction

High-quality content also involves interacting with your audience. Engaging with your viewers through comments, polls, and community posts fosters a sense of connection and helps build a loyal following. Responding to comments, acknowledging viewer feedback, and incorporating their suggestions into your videos not only strengthens your relationship with your audience but also helps create a more inclusive community around your content. Brands take notice of creators who have an engaged and active audience, as it indicates that the creator's influence can have a positive impact on potential customers.

Consistency in Uploading

One of the key factors in building and maintaining an engaged audience is consistency. Uploading content regularly helps keep your channel active and ensures that viewers can rely on you for fresh content. Consistency does not mean you need to upload daily, but having a clear schedule, whether it's weekly or bi-weekly, gives your audience something to look forward to. A consistent content schedule also helps boost your channel's visibility, as YouTube tends to favour active channels that upload regularly. Sponsors also appreciate consistent creators, as it provides them with a predictable platform to promote their products.

Value for the Audience

Your content must provide value to your viewers. This value can come in many forms, such as entertainment, education, inspiration, or practical tips. Understanding what your audience is looking for and consistently delivering value is one of the best ways to build a loyal community. When your audience finds your content helpful, interesting, or entertaining, they are more likely to return and recommend your videos to others. This, in turn, increases your channel's reach and makes you more attractive to potential sponsors. Brands want to collaborate with creators whose content speaks directly to their target audience, providing them with real value.

Optimisation for Search and Discovery

High-quality content also includes making your videos discoverable by optimising them for search. This involves using relevant keywords in your video title, description, and tags to ensure your content appears in search results when viewers are looking for related topics. A good thumbnail, a well-written video description, and attention-grabbing titles can help make your videos more clickable. YouTube's algorithm rewards videos that attract high engagement, so optimising your content for search can help boost your visibility and attract more viewers, which is a key factor in securing sponsorships.

How High-Quality Content Attracts Sponsors

Sponsors want to partner with creators who can produce content that reflects positively on their brand. By consistently uploading well-produced, engaging content, you demonstrate your professionalism and commitment to quality. This builds trust with sponsors, making them more likely to approach you for collaborations.

Moreover, high-quality content with a well-defined niche and engaged audience is highly attractive to sponsors. When your content resonates with your target audience and generates high engagement, sponsors see an opportunity to reach their ideal customers. The more professional your content appears, the more valuable your channel becomes to potential sponsors.

Conclusion

Creating high-quality content is one of the most important factors for achieving long-term success on YouTube. Not only does it attract and retain viewers, but it also increases your appeal to potential sponsors. By focusing on compelling storytelling, professional production, audience engagement, and consistency, you can create content that stands out and resonates with both viewers and brands. When you produce valuable, high-quality videos, you demonstrate your ability to generate meaningful engagement, which is crucial for securing lucrative sponsorship opportunities. As your content improves and your brand grows, you'll find that high-quality content becomes the foundation of your YouTube success.

Chapter-04

Engage with Your Audience: Foster a loyal community through interactions, responding to comments, and creating content based on their interests.

In the world of YouTube, engaging with your audience is one of the most powerful tools for building a successful channel. While creating high-quality content is important, fostering a loyal community through consistent interaction and meaningful connections takes your channel to the next level. Engaging with your audience not only increases viewer retention and encourages growth, but it also strengthens the relationship between you and your viewers, which can lead to greater success and opportunities, including lucrative sponsorships.

The Importance of Audience Engagement

Audience engagement is more than just responding to comments or liking posts; it's about building a community of people who feel valued, connected, and heard. When you take the time to interact with your viewers, they feel like they are a part of something bigger and that their opinions matter. This creates a deeper sense of loyalty and encourages viewers to continue following your channel, interact with your content, and share it with others.

For creators, this interaction is also vital in shaping content that resonates with your audience. By responding to feedback and understanding what your viewers like or dislike, you can tailor your videos to better suit their interests, improving the overall quality and relevance of your channel. Furthermore, a highly engaged audience is more likely to support you when it comes to monetising your content, whether through Super Chats, merchandise sales, or partnerships with sponsors.

How to Effectively Engage with Your Audience

Responding to Comments and Questions

One of the simplest and most direct ways to engage with your audience is by responding to comments. Viewers appreciate when a creator takes the time to acknowledge their input, whether it's a question, a compliment, or constructive feedback. Responding to comments shows that you value your audience's opinions and helps build a sense of connection. Engaging with your viewers in the comments section also encourages further interaction, as people are more likely to leave comments if they feel their contributions will be noticed and appreciated.

You don't have to respond to every comment, but showing that you read and care about what your viewers say can significantly improve your relationship with them. Personalising your responses and adding thoughtful replies can help foster a stronger sense of community.

Using Social Media to Foster Interaction

YouTube is not the only platform where you can interact with your audience. Leveraging social media platforms like Instagram, Twitter, TikTok, and Facebook can help you engage with your viewers on a more personal level. Social media allows you to share behind-the-scenes content, post updates about your channel, or hold Q&A sessions, giving your audience an insight into your life beyond your videos.

By engaging with your audience on different platforms, you can strengthen your relationship with them and attract new viewers to your YouTube channel. Social media also provides a great opportunity to start conversations, ask for feedback, and conduct polls to gauge your audience's preferences, which can directly inform the content you create.

Creating Interactive Content

Interactive content encourages viewers to engage with your videos in a more active way. This can include asking questions in your videos, prompting viewers to leave comments, or hosting live streams where you can directly interact with your audience in real time. Calls to action, such as asking your viewers to share their thoughts or experiences related to the video topic, can also increase engagement.

Live streaming is particularly effective in creating a direct connection with your audience. You can interact with viewers through real-time comments, answer questions, and engage in live discussions. This creates a sense of exclusivity and intimacy, making viewers feel like they are a part of the conversation. Live Q&A sessions, giveaways, and challenges are great ways to encourage active participation and deepen viewer engagement.

Acknowledging Your Community

Another important aspect of audience engagement is recognising and acknowledging the people who support you. Mentioning loyal subscribers in your videos, thanking your audience for reaching milestones, or celebrating key moments together creates a sense of community. When viewers feel recognised for their support, they are more likely to stay engaged with your content and continue interacting with your channel.

Celebrating your audience's achievements, such as highlighting their comments or featuring their suggestions, shows that you are not just a creator, but also a part of a larger community. This inclusivity can help build stronger, more meaningful connections with your viewers.

Requesting and Incorporating Viewer Feedback

One of the most effective ways to create content that resonates with your audience is by directly involving them in the content creation process. By asking your viewers what they want to see or requesting feedback on previous videos, you show that their opinions matter to you. Incorporating their suggestions into your content not only makes your audience feel valued but also improves the relevance and quality of your videos.

For example, you can ask your viewers to vote on topics for future videos through polls or surveys on social media or YouTube's community tab. You can also ask them to share their experiences, opinions, or ideas in the comments, and then create videos that respond to their feedback. By making your viewers feel like they have an active role in shaping your content, you build a more loyal and engaged audience.

Create Exclusive Content for Loyal Followers

Offering exclusive content or rewards for your most loyal followers can further strengthen engagement. This can include providing early access to videos, behind-the-scenes footage, exclusive live streams, or offering a Patreon or membership program where viewers can support you financially in exchange for special perks.

Exclusive content makes your viewers feel appreciated and more connected to you as a creator. It also incentivises them to stay engaged with your content and continue supporting your channel. Loyal followers are more likely to share your content, recommend your channel to others, and become ambassadors for your brand.

The Benefits of Audience Engagement for YouTube Success

Building a Loyal Community

Consistent interaction with your audience helps build a loyal community that feels connected to you. Loyal followers are more likely to return to your videos, engage with your content, and recommend your channel to others. This community becomes the foundation of your channel's success and provides ongoing support, which is crucial for sustained growth.

Increased Engagement and Reach

Engagement is a critical factor in YouTube's algorithm. Channels with higher engagement rates—such as likes, comments, shares, and subscriptions—are more likely to be recommended by the platform. A highly engaged audience also increases the likelihood of your videos being shared across social media, further expanding your reach.

Attracting Sponsors

Brands want to work with creators who have an engaged and loyal audience. By interacting with your viewers and creating content based on their interests, you demonstrate that you understand your audience and can generate meaningful engagement. Sponsors are more likely to collaborate with creators who have a proven track record of engaging with their community and producing content that resonates with their target market.

Conclusion

Engaging with your audience is a key component of building a successful YouTube channel. By fostering a loyal community through interactions, responding to comments, and creating content based on your viewers' interests, you create a strong bond with your audience that encourages ongoing support. Audience engagement not only leads to higher viewer retention and increased reach but also makes your channel more appealing to potential sponsors. As your community grows, so too does the opportunity for greater success on YouTube. By prioritising engagement, you lay the foundation for long-term growth, a thriving community, and more lucrative partnerships.

Chapter-05

Reach a Solid Subscriber Count: While large numbers aren't everything, a solid, engaged audience is crucial to attracting the right sponsors.

Building a solid subscriber count is essential for growing your YouTube channel and attracting the right sponsors. While large numbers can be appealing, they aren't the be-all and end-all when it comes to success. A smaller but highly engaged and dedicated audience can be more valuable to potential sponsors than a massive but passive following. Sponsors are increasingly looking for creators with genuine, loyal viewers who interact with their content regularly and fit their target demographic. For YouTube creators, reaching a solid subscriber count with engaged viewers is the key to unlocking new opportunities, including lucrative sponsorship deals.

Why Subscriber Count Matters

Subscribers are a clear indicator of your channel's popularity and growth potential. A solid subscriber count suggests that people find value in your content and are committed to returning for more. These subscribers are more likely to watch your videos, engage with them through likes, comments, and shares, and spread the word about your channel to others. This consistent engagement is crucial for increasing your channel's visibility on YouTube's algorithm, which favours content that generates high levels of interaction.

Moreover, a strong subscriber count increases your channel's credibility. When potential sponsors view your channel, they want to see that you have an active audience that is interested in what you have to offer. A high number of subscribers demonstrates that you have created content that resonates with viewers and that your channel has the potential to reach even wider audiences.

However, it's important to note that simply having a large subscriber count is not enough. Sponsors are more interested in the engagement rate, meaning how actively your audience interacts with your videos. Channels with a high engagement rate are often more attractive to brands, as they provide an opportunity to reach a dedicated and responsive audience.

The Difference Between Subscribers and Engagement

While your subscriber count is an important metric, the engagement level of your audience often holds more value when attracting sponsors. Engagement refers to the actions your viewers take while watching your videos, such as liking, commenting, sharing, and clicking on links or calls to action. A smaller but highly engaged audience is more likely to trust your opinions, take action on your sponsored promotions, and support your channel financially through memberships or donations.

It's possible to have a large number of subscribers but still struggle with low engagement. This can happen if subscribers aren't actively interacting with your content or if the content no longer resonates with them. For this reason, sponsors tend to prioritise engagement over pure subscriber numbers. They want to partner with creators whose audiences are not only large but also consistently interact with the content in a meaningful way.

On the other hand, a solid subscriber count coupled with strong engagement means your audience is not only watching your videos but also genuinely interested in what you have to say. This creates a fertile environment for sponsorships, as brands are more confident that your audience will respond to their products and services.

How to Build a Solid Subscriber Count

Create Consistent, High-Quality Content

The foundation of growing a solid subscriber count is consistently uploading high-quality content. Viewers are more likely to subscribe to a channel that regularly provides value, whether it's through entertainment, education, or inspiration. When your content is aligned with your audience's interests, it encourages them to hit the subscribe button and return for more.

Consistency is crucial when building a subscriber base. Uploading regularly, whether it's once a week or bi-weekly, keeps your audience engaged and gives them something to look forward to. Regular uploads also signal to YouTube's algorithm that your channel is active, which can help your videos get more exposure and attract new subscribers.

Engage with Your Viewers

Building a loyal and engaged audience is just as important as increasing your subscriber count. By interacting with your viewers through comments, social media, and live streams, you foster a sense of community and make your subscribers feel valued. This connection encourages them to stay subscribed and engage more actively with your content.

Creating content that directly responds to viewer comments or feedback is another way to encourage engagement. For example, if your viewers ask for specific types of content or have suggestions, incorporating their ideas into your videos shows that you care about their input, which strengthens the relationship and keeps them invested in your channel.

Promote Your Channel Across Platforms

To grow your subscriber count, it's important to promote your content outside of YouTube. Social media platforms like Instagram, Twitter, Facebook, and TikTok offer great opportunities to reach new audiences and direct them to your YouTube channel. You can share snippets of your videos, behind-the-scenes content, and personal updates to create interest in your channel and encourage people to subscribe.

Additionally, collaborations with other creators can help expose your channel to new viewers who may be interested in your content. When you collaborate with other creators in your niche, you tap into their audience, which can help you grow your subscriber base more rapidly.

Use Calls to Action

Encouraging viewers to subscribe is often as simple as asking them to do so. A clear and friendly call to action (CTA) in your videos, such as "Don't forget to subscribe for more content," can remind viewers to hit the subscribe button. However, it's important not to overdo it—CTAs should feel natural and be placed in a way that adds value to the viewer's experience. For example, you can mention subscribing after sharing valuable content or at the end of the video when viewers are more likely to commit to it.

Offer Value and Incentives

Offering value to your viewers increases the chances that they will subscribe to your channel. This value can come in many forms, such as educational content, entertainment, or insights into a particular niche. By establishing yourself as an expert in your field or providing unique content, you make it clear to potential subscribers why they should follow your channel.

Additionally, offering incentives such as exclusive content, giveaways, or early access to videos can entice viewers to subscribe and stay engaged. These incentives reward your audience for their loyalty and create a sense of exclusivity that encourages more viewers to join your subscriber base.

The Role of Subscribers in Attracting Sponsors

When you have a solid subscriber count, especially one that's paired with high engagement, you increase your appeal to potential sponsors. Brands are more likely to approach creators who have a proven ability to generate views, build a community, and maintain strong viewer interaction. A healthy subscriber base with consistent engagement gives sponsors the confidence that their product will reach a dedicated audience.

Moreover, having a loyal and engaged audience provides opportunities for monetisation through sponsorships, product placements, affiliate marketing, and merchandise sales. Sponsors want to partner with creators who can not only reach a large number of viewers but who also have an audience that trusts their recommendations and is likely to take action.

Conclusion

While reaching a large number of subscribers is important, a solid, engaged subscriber base is the true key to success on YouTube. Subscribers who actively engage with your content are more likely to return, share your videos, and become ambassadors for your brand. By focusing on building a loyal and engaged community through consistent content, interaction, and value, you can attract the right sponsors who are looking for creators with genuine influence and an audience that aligns with their brand. Reaching a solid subscriber count not only boosts your credibility but also increases the potential for lucrative sponsorships and long-term success on YouTube.

Chapter-06

Have a Professional Media Kit: A well-designed media kit showcasing your statistics, audience demographics, and past brand collaborations can make a powerful impression.

In the competitive world of YouTube, a professional media kit is an essential tool for creators looking to attract brand partnerships and sponsorships. A well-crafted media kit provides potential sponsors with a comprehensive snapshot of your channel, your audience, and your previous collaborations. It serves as a powerful marketing document that highlights your value as a content creator and demonstrates why brands should consider partnering with you. By showcasing your statistics, audience demographics, and past brand collaborations, a media kit can make a lasting impression and help you secure lucrative sponsorship deals.

What is a Media Kit?

A media kit is essentially a digital portfolio that outlines key details about your YouTube channel. It serves as a resource for potential sponsors to better understand your reach, audience, and influence. Typically, a media kit includes information about your channel's performance, such as subscriber count, average views per video, engagement rate, audience demographics, and any notable collaborations or partnerships you've previously had. It's a way to professionally present yourself and your channel to brands, showing them how partnering with you can benefit their marketing efforts.

Having a media kit is an essential step in professionalising your brand. Without one, you may miss out on opportunities because potential sponsors may not have a clear understanding of what you offer or how your channel aligns with their target audience. A media kit helps you stand out from the competition by making it easier for brands to assess the value you bring to the table.

Key Components of a Media Kit

Channel Overview and Introduction

Your media kit should begin with an introduction to your channel, including a brief summary of who you are, the type of content you create, and what makes you unique. This section is your opportunity to tell potential sponsors about your mission, values, and creative vision. You can also mention any niche you specialise in, such as beauty, fitness, gaming, or lifestyle, to help brands understand if your content aligns with their product or service.
Additionally, highlight what sets you apart from other content creators. Whether it's your personality, the way you engage with your audience, or your creative approach, make sure to showcase what makes your channel special.

Audience Demographics

One of the most important aspects of your media kit is your audience demographics. Brands want to know who your viewers are, as they are looking to reach specific target audiences. Include detailed information about the age, gender, location, and interests of your audience. Tools such as YouTube Analytics can provide you with valuable insights into who is watching your videos, allowing you to present this information in

a clear, concise way.
For example, if your audience is predominantly young adults between 18-24 years old, this could be appealing to brands targeting this age group. Similarly, if you have a global following, be sure to highlight key regions where your audience is based, as this can help brands determine if your viewers are in markets they want to reach.

Channel Statistics

A key element of your media kit is showcasing your channel's performance statistics. This includes your total number of subscribers, views per video, average engagement rate, and overall video performance. It's also beneficial to show any significant growth trends, such as an increase in subscribers or views over a particular period. These statistics help potential sponsors gauge the reach and effectiveness of your channel. For example, if your videos consistently generate a high level of engagement, it shows that your audience is actively interacting with your content, which is an attractive proposition for brands. The more impressive and consistent your statistics are, the more likely you are to attract sponsorship deals.

Past Brand Collaborations and Testimonials

Including details about any previous brand collaborations can greatly enhance your media kit. Highlight successful campaigns where you've worked with brands, showcasing the impact of your partnership. Be sure to mention any notable brands you've collaborated with, as well as the outcomes of those partnerships—such as the number of views, click-through rates, or sales generated through affiliate links.
If you have testimonials from brands or companies you've worked with, include these as well. Positive feedback from past partners serves as social proof, reinforcing your ability to deliver results and making your media kit more persuasive. If you don't have many collaborations yet, consider including examples of smaller or personal brand projects to show your experience in working with brands, even if they weren't major partnerships.

Content Opportunities and Packages

Your media kit should also outline the types of content you offer for brand collaborations. This could include sponsored videos, product placements, brand mentions, social media shout-outs, giveaways, or affiliate marketing. Provide details on how you can integrate a brand's product or service into your content in a natural and engaging way.
It's also helpful to present pricing packages for these opportunities. Some creators prefer to keep this information private until they engage in negotiations, but having a pricing structure can make it easier for brands to understand what they are paying for and what they can expect in return. Make sure to be transparent about your rates and what each package includes.

Visual Branding and Design

The design of your media kit is just as important as its content. A clean, professional design that aligns with your channel's aesthetic can make a significant difference in how it's received by potential sponsors. Use high-quality images, branded colours, and fonts that reflect your style. A visually appealing media kit conveys professionalism and can help leave a lasting impression on brands.
You can also include screenshots of your YouTube channel, video thumbnails, or even highlights from your most popular videos to give sponsors a visual sense of your content. This helps them get a feel for your style and the type of audience you attract.

Why a Media Kit is Essential for Attracting Sponsors

A media kit serves as your channel's business card, providing potential sponsors with all the information they need to make an informed decision. By presenting a well-organised and visually appealing kit, you show that you take your content creation seriously and are capable of managing brand collaborations professionally. A solid media kit can also help you stand out from the competition, as not all creators take the time to craft one.

Sponsors are looking for creators who can help them reach their target market in an authentic way. A media kit allows you to demonstrate how your audience aligns with their brand, showing that you can deliver measurable results. It's an opportunity to showcase your value and convince brands that partnering with you is a worthwhile investment.

Conclusion

A well-designed media kit is a powerful tool for attracting sponsors and monetising your YouTube channel. It provides a comprehensive overview of your channel's performance, audience demographics, and past collaborations, all of which are crucial for potential sponsors looking to evaluate the value of partnering with you. By presenting your statistics, audience insights, and professional design in a cohesive and organised way, you increase your chances of securing brand partnerships that will help you grow and monetise your content. Whether you're a new creator or an experienced one, investing time in crafting a media kit can make a significant impact on your success in the YouTube space.

Chapter-07

Understand Your Analytics: Use YouTube's analytics to demonstrate your reach, viewer demographics, and engagement rates to potential sponsors.

In the world of YouTube content creation, understanding and leveraging your analytics is crucial to attracting and securing sponsorships.

YouTube's analytics platform provides a wealth of data about your channel's performance, audience demographics, and engagement, which can be used to demonstrate your value to potential sponsors. By effectively interpreting and presenting this information, you can show brands that partnering with you offers a unique opportunity to reach a targeted and engaged audience.

The Importance of Analytics for Sponsors

YouTube analytics give creators a detailed view of how their content is performing and how their audience interacts with it. For potential sponsors, this data is vital in determining whether a partnership will be effective in reaching their target market. Brands are no longer looking solely at subscriber count—they want to understand your audience's preferences, behaviours, and the impact your videos have. They seek creators who have a dedicated and engaged following, and analytics help prove that.

By using YouTube's analytics, you can show sponsors that you are not only capable of producing content but that your audience actively engages with it. This data can directly influence sponsorship decisions, making it essential for creators to understand and effectively communicate their metrics.

Key Analytics Metrics to Showcase to Sponsors

Audience Demographics

One of the most important aspects of YouTube analytics is the demographic data it provides. This includes information about the age, gender, location, and interests of your audience. Sponsors are looking for creators whose audience matches their target demographic, so being able to present this information clearly and accurately can greatly

improve your chances of securing a partnership.
For instance, if your content is targeted towards young adults aged 18-34, brands selling products for this age group will be particularly interested. If you have a global audience, you can highlight which countries or regions have the highest number of viewers, which can help brands who are looking to expand into specific markets.
By presenting these demographics in an easily digestible format—such as charts or graphs—you can effectively show sponsors that your audience aligns with their marketing goals. If your viewers are largely based in specific cities or countries, or if they share certain interests, you can tailor your pitch to reflect how this targeted audience makes you an ideal partner for their brand.

Engagement Rate

Engagement rate is one of the most valuable metrics for demonstrating the effectiveness of your content. It measures how actively your audience interacts with your videos through likes, comments, shares, and click-through rates. YouTube analytics offers insights into the number of likes, comments, and shares each video receives, as well as the average view duration.
Sponsors are more interested in how much interaction a video generates rather than how many people simply view it. An engaged audience is more likely to trust the creator's recommendations, making them more likely to take action on sponsored content. If your videos have high engagement rates, it suggests that your audience is loyal, interested, and likely to respond positively to sponsored promotions.
YouTube also provides an "engagement" tab in its analytics, which shows how viewers are engaging with your content over time. This can be helpful when demonstrating the success of previous collaborations or the potential for future brand integrations.

Watch Time and Views

Total watch time and average views per video are critical for showcasing your channel's reach and impact. Watch time is a measure of how long viewers spend watching your videos, and it plays a major role in YouTube's algorithm. A high watch time indicates that your content is holding the attention of your audience and that they are interested in watching multiple videos, which is an appealing factor for sponsors.

Average views per video is another important metric that shows how many people are consistently watching your content. While subscriber count is important, potential sponsors are more focused on the real-time performance of your videos. High viewership, especially if those views come from a targeted audience, can make your channel a highly attractive option for brands.

By demonstrating strong watch time and views in your analytics, you show sponsors that your content has the reach and ability to generate exposure for their brand. YouTube also allows you to break down views by specific videos, so you can highlight those that performed particularly well or that had significant brand collaboration success.

Audience Retention

Audience retention is a metric that shows how long people continue watching your videos before they click away. High audience retention means that viewers are watching your videos for longer periods, indicating that your content is both engaging and valuable to them. This is important for sponsors because it demonstrates that your content has the power to capture attention and keep it for extended periods, making your channel an ideal place for sponsored promotions.

YouTube provides detailed retention graphs, showing where viewers drop off during a video. By analysing these trends, you can also refine your content strategy to increase retention, which in turn boosts the attractiveness of your channel for potential sponsors. A high retention rate is a clear indicator of quality content, which is something that brands want to associate with their products.

Traffic Sources

Knowing where your traffic is coming from is crucial for understanding your audience's behaviour. YouTube analytics breaks down traffic sources into categories such as YouTube search, external websites, social media, and suggested videos. This information can help you demonstrate how your audience is finding and engaging with your content.

For sponsors, knowing where your traffic comes from can help them assess how their brand will be exposed to different groups of people. For instance, if a significant portion of your traffic comes from social media, it suggests that your followers are actively sharing your content with their networks, increasing its potential reach.

By showing that your content is being discovered and shared through multiple channels, you increase your appeal to brands looking to maximise their exposure.

Top Performing Videos

YouTube's analytics also provide insights into which of your videos are performing the best in terms of views, engagement, and watch time. By highlighting your top-performing videos, you can show sponsors which content resonates most with your audience. This is especially helpful if those videos feature content similar to what the brand is looking for or if they have been successful in past collaborations.

Brands often want to see examples of how their products or services could be integrated into your content, so showing top-performing videos can give them a clear sense of what kind of results they might expect.

How to Present Your Analytics to Potential Sponsors

When presenting your YouTube analytics to potential sponsors, it's essential to present the information in a clear and visually appealing way. Use graphs, charts, and screenshots to make the data easy to digest. Rather than overwhelming sponsors with raw data, focus on key metrics that demonstrate your value—such as audience demographics, engagement rates, and watch time.

By providing sponsors with a clear overview of your channel's performance and audience, you can effectively demonstrate that your channel is a valuable platform for brand partnerships. Use these insights to show how your audience aligns with their target demographic and how your content can generate exposure for their products.

Conclusion

Understanding and using YouTube's analytics is essential for content creators looking to attract sponsors. By showcasing key metrics such as audience demographics, engagement rates, watch time, and traffic sources, you can provide potential sponsors with a compelling case for why they should partner with you. Your analytics offer a detailed view of your channel's reach and influence, which, when presented effectively, can demonstrate your value to brands and help you secure valuable sponsorship opportunities.

Chapter-08

Showcase Your Value Proposition: Brands want to know how working with you will benefit them. Be clear about the value you bring.

When approaching potential sponsors, it's crucial to clearly communicate your value proposition—the unique benefits you offer to brands. Sponsors want to know how collaborating with you will help them achieve their marketing goals. A strong value proposition is not just about showcasing your channel's reach or popularity, but about demonstrating how your content and audience can drive results for the brands you work with. This means articulating how your unique characteristics, content style, and audience engagement will benefit the sponsor's brand and objectives.

What is a Value Proposition?

A value proposition is a statement or concept that explains the value a product or service will deliver to customers, highlighting why it is different from competitors. In the context of YouTube, your value proposition is about clearly explaining why a brand should invest in sponsoring your channel over others. It encompasses your content's appeal, your audience's characteristics, your credibility, and your ability to drive engagement and sales.

Brands are looking for more than just a large audience—they want to know that their message will resonate with the right people, and that you can effectively integrate their products into your content in a way that drives interest, engagement, and action. To create a compelling value proposition, you must highlight the unique aspects of your channel, explain how it aligns with the brand's goals, and demonstrate how you can deliver measurable results.

Why Sponsors Care About Your Value Proposition

Sponsors are looking for content creators who can help them meet specific objectives, whether that's raising brand awareness, boosting sales, or promoting a new product. A clear value proposition helps them see how your channel can support those goals.

Reaching the Right Audience

Brands don't just want exposure—they want to reach the right audience. Your value proposition should highlight your niche and demonstrate how your audience aligns with the sponsor's target market. For example, if your channel focuses on health and wellness, and the brand sells fitness products, your audience will likely consist of individuals interested in health, fitness, and wellbeing. This makes your channel an

ideal platform for promoting their products.
Providing detailed information about your audience demographics—such as age, gender, location, and interests—helps brands assess whether you are the right fit for their campaign. If you have an engaged and loyal community that shares interests that match the brand's, this will strengthen your value proposition.

Engagement and Relationship with Your Audience

Engagement is another key factor that sponsors consider. They want to know that your audience isn't just watching your content passively, but actively engaging with it. High levels of interaction through likes, comments, shares, and direct feedback are indicators that your viewers trust and value your content. Sponsors want to partner with creators whose audiences are not only large but also genuinely invested in the content.

Your value proposition should emphasise your relationship with your viewers. Highlight the ways in which you foster community and engage with your audience through comments, live chats, polls, and other forms of interaction. If your viewers trust your opinions and engage with your content regularly, it shows that they are more likely to act on product recommendations, making your platform even more attractive to sponsors.

Content Quality and Creativity

Another aspect of your value proposition is the quality of your content. Brands want to collaborate with creators who produce content that is well-crafted, professional, and engaging. This is where you can showcase your skills in storytelling, video production, and creativity. If your content consistently resonates with viewers, whether it's through informative videos, entertainment, or product reviews, you are demonstrating that you have the ability to create content that attracts attention. Highlight any special skills or techniques that set your videos apart from others, such as your editing style, humour, storytelling approach, or the unique angle you take on a topic. These elements of your content are what make your channel stand out, and they are a key part of your value proposition to potential sponsors.

Proven Track Record of Success

To make your value proposition even more compelling, it's essential to back up your claims with proof. Sponsors are more likely to invest in creators who have a track record of success. Highlight past brand collaborations and the results they delivered. If you have successfully promoted products or services in previous campaigns, demonstrate how your content led to measurable outcomes—such as increased views, higher engagement, or sales conversions.

Case studies or testimonials from previous sponsors are particularly effective here. By providing concrete evidence of the success of past campaigns, you reassure potential sponsors that you are capable of delivering results. This also positions you as a professional who understands the business side of content creation and is able to manage brand partnerships effectively.

Authenticity and Credibility

In today's market, authenticity is highly valued by both audiences and brands. Sponsors want to work with creators who genuinely believe in the products or services they promote, as this comes across as more credible and relatable to viewers. Your value proposition should highlight your authenticity and how you integrate sponsorships into your content in an organic way.

If you have built a reputation for being trustworthy and transparent, this can be a significant selling point. For example, if you only promote products or brands that align with your values and content, this demonstrates to sponsors that your endorsement will come across as genuine and not forced. The more authentic your partnership with a brand appears, the more likely your audience is to engage with the content and act on the sponsor's message.

Delivering Return on Investment (ROI)

Ultimately, brands want to see a return on their investment. Your value proposition should emphasise how your content can help sponsors achieve their objectives. Whether it's increasing brand awareness, generating leads, or driving sales, it's important to outline how you can deliver measurable results.

Demonstrating your ROI can be done through previous success stories, audience data, or any other metrics that show how your content has helped brands meet their goals. For example, if you've worked with a brand in the past and saw a boost in traffic to their website or an increase in sales through an affiliate link, this data should be included in your value proposition to show the potential benefits for future sponsors.

Crafting Your Value Proposition: Key Elements to Include

When crafting your value proposition, it's important to make sure it is clear, concise, and targeted. A strong value proposition includes the following elements:

A clear understanding of your niche and audience – Show how your content aligns with the brand's target market.

High engagement rates – Demonstrate the trust and loyalty of your audience.

Content quality and creativity – Highlight what sets your content apart from others in your niche.

Proven success with previous collaborations – Share past campaigns and measurable results.

Authenticity and credibility – Emphasise how your partnerships will feel genuine and resonate with your audience.

Potential for ROI – Make it clear how you can help the sponsor achieve their goals.

Conclusion

Showcasing your value proposition is crucial for attracting sponsors on YouTube. It's about more than just having a large following; it's about clearly communicating the unique value you offer and how you can help brands achieve their marketing goals. By highlighting your audience, engagement, content quality, authenticity, and proven success, you can craft a compelling value proposition that will convince sponsors that working with you is a worthwhile investment. When done right, a strong value proposition can make you an attractive partner for brands, leading to lucrative collaborations and long-term partnerships.

Chapter-09

Reach Out to Brands: Don't wait for brands to come to you. Proactively reach out with a pitch tailored to their needs and values.

In the competitive world of YouTube content creation, waiting for brands to approach you may not always yield the best results. While large brands may occasionally reach out to top creators, smaller and niche brands are often seeking creators who fit their needs but may not know about you yet. Therefore, it is important to take the initiative and actively reach out to potential sponsors. Crafting a thoughtful, well-targeted pitch tailored to a brand's needs and values can set you apart from the crowd and lead to valuable collaborations.

Why You Should Reach Out to Brands

Proactively reaching out to brands shows initiative and demonstrates your professionalism. Brands appreciate creators who take the time to research their products and propose partnerships that align with their objectives. By contacting a brand directly, you have the opportunity to craft a personalised pitch that highlights how your content can help them achieve their marketing goals, whether that's increasing awareness, driving sales, or engaging a specific audience. A well-targeted outreach shows you are not just waiting for opportunities to fall into your lap but are actively working to build mutually beneficial relationships.

Moreover, reaching out allows you to be more selective with the brands you choose to work with. You can identify businesses that align with your niche, audience, and values, leading to more authentic partnerships that resonate with both your viewers and the brand's target market. This tailored approach will ultimately result in more successful and long-term sponsorships.

Steps for Effectively Reaching Out to Brands

Research the Brand and Its Goals

Before reaching out to a brand, it's essential to do thorough research. Understand the brand's products, values, and target audience. This information will help you tailor your pitch to address how you can specifically help them achieve their goals. For example, if the brand is focused on sustainability, highlight how your content or audience aligns with eco-friendly values. If the brand's product is aimed at fitness enthusiasts, you could discuss how your channel's health and wellness content aligns with their market.

By demonstrating an understanding of the brand's goals and challenges, you show that you are not just interested in a sponsorship for financial gain, but that you are genuinely invested in helping the brand succeed. Personalising your pitch in this way shows professionalism and increases your chances of success.

Craft a Compelling Pitch

Your pitch should be clear, concise, and persuasive. Start by introducing yourself and explaining why you're interested in working with the brand. Be specific about why you think the collaboration would be a good fit. Use the research you've conducted to highlight how your audience aligns with their target demographic and how your content style matches their brand ethos. If you've worked with other brands in the past, include relevant case studies or examples of past collaborations to demonstrate your track record of success.

When crafting your pitch, focus on the value you bring to the brand. Explain how you can help them achieve their goals, whether it's through raising brand awareness, driving sales, or engaging with a specific audience. Emphasise your unique selling points, such as your niche, audience engagement, or the quality of your content. Make it clear how working with you will benefit the brand and show that you've thought about how their product will integrate into your content in a natural and engaging way.

Be Clear About What You're Offering

Your pitch should include a clear outline of what you are offering in the partnership. Whether you are proposing a one-off sponsored video, a series of posts, or a long-term collaboration, be transparent about what the brand can expect in terms of deliverables. Provide a brief but detailed overview of your content strategy, including the types of videos you plan to create, how you will feature the product, and any other relevant details such as post frequency, social media promotion, or affiliate links.

It's also helpful to include information about your audience demographics, engagement rates, and any other analytics that demonstrate the potential reach and impact of your content. This will help brands understand the value of partnering with you and give them a sense of the return on investment they can expect from the collaboration.

Be Professional and Personable

When reaching out to brands, your communication should strike a balance between professionalism and friendliness. While it's important to be respectful and formal in your approach, it's also essential to convey enthusiasm and passion for their brand and products. Brands want to work with creators who are not only professional but also excited about their product, as this enthusiasm translates to more genuine and effective promotions.

Address the brand by name, personalise your email or message to reflect your knowledge of their product or company, and be polite in your tone. Always ensure that your pitch is free from errors and that you present yourself in a polished and credible manner. Remember, first impressions count, so it's important to convey professionalism from the outset.

Follow Up

After sending your initial pitch, it's important to follow up. Brands receive numerous inquiries, so a follow-up message can help keep you top of mind. Wait around a week or two before following up with a polite, concise email. Reiterate your interest in working with the brand and inquire if they had the chance to review your proposal. If they haven't responded yet, express your continued interest and ask if they need any further information.

A follow-up not only shows persistence but also helps demonstrate your commitment and interest in a potential partnership. However, it's important to remain courteous and not to overdo it. If a brand hasn't responded after a couple of follow-ups, it's wise to move on and focus on other opportunities.

Be Flexible and Open to Negotiation

When brands show interest in collaborating, be open to discussions about terms, deliverables, and compensation. Flexibility is key, as each brand may have different needs or preferences. Some brands may prefer a longer-term partnership, while others may be interested in a single campaign. Be prepared to negotiate on details such as payment, video format, and content expectations. Having a clear understanding of your own value and the type of partnership you want is important, but being open to negotiation can help you build successful relationships with brands.

If you're new to brand outreach or don't have extensive experience in negotiating deals, it's helpful to seek advice from other creators or professionals who can guide you through the process.

How to Stand Out in a Crowded Market

In a competitive market, standing out is crucial to securing sponsorships. One way to do this is by showcasing the unique aspects of your channel and your content. If you have a niche audience, such as a focus on a particular hobby, lifestyle, or interest, use that as a selling point. Highlight the quality of your content, your audience's loyalty, and the authentic connection you have with them.

It's also important to demonstrate that you understand the brand's objectives and that you're committed to delivering results. By being proactive, professional, and focused on the value you can provide, you differentiate yourself from other creators who may be waiting for brands to reach out.

Conclusion

Reaching out to brands and proactively pitching your channel for sponsorship opportunities is an essential part of building successful brand collaborations on YouTube. By researching potential sponsors, crafting a tailored pitch, and being clear about the value you bring, you can increase your chances of securing meaningful partnerships. A personalised, well-crafted pitch shows brands that you are not only professional but also genuinely invested in helping them achieve their marketing objectives. By taking the initiative, you open doors to a wider range of sponsorship opportunities and position yourself as a proactive, results-driven creator.

Chapter-10

Negotiate Fairly: Ensure that you are compensated fairly for your work, keeping in mind both your time and the exposure you're providing the brand.

Negotiating fair compensation for brand collaborations is an essential skill for YouTube creators. While many creators may be excited about the opportunity to work with brands, it's important to remember that your time, expertise, and audience reach are valuable. You are providing a service that helps brands promote their products, and just as with any other business partnership, you should be compensated fairly for your work. Negotiating effectively ensures that you are rewarded for the effort you put into content creation and the exposure you provide to the brand, while also setting a standard for the value of your work.

Why Fair Negotiation is Important

Fair negotiation is crucial for several reasons. Firstly, it sets the foundation for a sustainable and professional relationship between you and the brand. If you accept offers that undervalue your time or content, it may create frustration and resentment, potentially damaging future partnerships. Secondly, being compensated fairly allows you to reinvest in your channel, improving the quality of your content, increasing your reach, and enhancing your value to future sponsors.

Neglecting fair compensation can also undermine your credibility as a creator. If other brands or creators perceive that you're undervaluing your work, it may signal to them that you are not taking your career seriously. On the other hand, negotiating fairly demonstrates that you understand the worth of your content and are committed to running a professional, sustainable business. This helps to build respect within the industry and fosters long-term partnerships.

Know Your Worth

The first step in negotiating fairly is understanding your worth. Many creators, especially those new to sponsorships, may undervalue their services or feel uncomfortable asking for what they deserve. However, to negotiate effectively, you need to have a clear sense of the value you provide to brands.

Your worth as a creator is not solely defined by the number of subscribers or views you have. While audience size plays a role, other factors such as audience engagement, niche, content quality, and your ability to create compelling and authentic brand integrations are equally important. A smaller but highly engaged audience can be far more valuable than a larger, less active one. Brands are willing to pay for the exposure and credibility you bring, as well as the opportunity to reach their target market through your unique content.

Research Industry Rates

Before entering into a negotiation, it's essential to research the typical industry rates for creators of your size and niche. Rates for sponsored content can vary significantly depending on factors such as your subscriber count, views per video, engagement rate, and the complexity of the deliverables. While rates are not always transparent, you can find useful benchmarks through creator communities, industry reports, or networking with other creators who have experience in brand deals.

There are also online platforms that can provide insight into how much brands are paying for YouTube sponsorships in your niche. This research helps you set realistic expectations and avoid undervaluing your work. Being knowledgeable about industry standards enables you to approach negotiations with confidence and ensure that the compensation you are offered is in line with the market.

Consider the Full Value of the Deal

When negotiating with a brand, it's important to consider the full value of the deal, not just the upfront payment. While direct financial compensation is a significant part of the negotiation, there are other factors that contribute to the overall value of the partnership. These can include:

Exposure

A brand may offer additional exposure through cross-promotion on their social media channels, website, or email newsletters. This can significantly extend the reach of your content and attract new subscribers.

Free Products or Services

Some brands may offer free products or services as part of the deal. While this may not be a direct financial gain, it can still hold value, particularly if the products align with your content and audience interests. Consider how the products or services fit into your channel's content and how they could be leveraged in future videos.

Long-term Partnerships

In some cases, a brand may offer a long-term partnership rather than a one-off collaboration. These arrangements can provide more stable and predictable income streams. Ensure you negotiate terms that are mutually beneficial and reflect the ongoing nature of the partnership.

Performance-based Incentives

Some brands may offer performance-based compensation, such as commissions or bonuses based on the number of sales generated from affiliate links or discount codes. Be sure to assess the potential for earnings from these incentives, and ensure that the terms are clear and fair.

By evaluating the overall value of the deal, you can ensure that you're not simply focusing on one aspect, such as payment, but are taking a more holistic view of the partnership.

Be Clear About Deliverables and Expectations

Clear communication is key to a successful negotiation. Ensure that both you and the brand have a mutual understanding of the deliverables and expectations for the campaign. This includes the type of content, the frequency of posts, deadlines, and the level of involvement the brand expects from you.

For example, if the brand expects you to create a series of videos, make sure the scope of the work is clearly outlined in the agreement. If you are asked to mention their product in a video, clarify how prominently it will be featured and whether the brand will have any input into the content. Setting clear expectations from the outset prevents misunderstandings and ensures that both parties are satisfied with the results.

Also, be realistic about what you can deliver. Don't agree to excessive or unrealistic demands in order to secure a deal. It's important to know your limits and ensure that the work required fits within your capacity as a creator.

Negotiating Payment

One of the most important aspects of any negotiation is payment. It's essential to ensure that the compensation reflects the value you're providing. This includes considering the time it will take to create the content, the exposure you'll be providing, and the potential long-term benefits for the brand.

When discussing payment, be clear about your rates and the basis for your pricing. If a brand offers less than your standard rate, don't be afraid to negotiate. If you believe that the offer doesn't reflect the value of your content, explain why you believe a higher rate is justified.

Sometimes brands may have budget constraints, but they may be open to negotiating in other ways, such as offering additional perks or expanding the scope of the deal.

Set Clear Contractual Terms

Once you've reached an agreement, it's essential to formalise the deal with a clear contract. A contract outlines the terms and conditions of the partnership, ensuring that both you and the brand are legally protected. The contract should include details about the compensation, deliverables, timelines, rights to content, and any additional terms such as exclusivity, non-disclosure agreements, and performance-based incentives.

Make sure to read the contract thoroughly before signing, and seek legal advice if necessary. A clear, well-drafted contract ensures that both parties understand their obligations and helps prevent misunderstandings or disputes in the future.

Conclusion

Negotiating fairly is a critical aspect of building successful brand partnerships. By understanding your worth, researching industry rates, and considering the full value of a deal, you can ensure that you are fairly compensated for the work you put into your content and the exposure you provide to brands. Clear communication, understanding your audience, and setting realistic expectations are essential for a successful negotiation. With the right approach, you can create long-term, mutually beneficial partnerships that not only support your growth as a creator but also ensure that you are treated as a professional in the industry.

Chapter-11

Build Long-Term Relationships: Rather than one-off deals, aim to establish lasting partnerships with brands that align with your values.

In the world of YouTube sponsorships, many creators focus on securing one-off brand deals, which can provide short-term gains. However, the most successful creators recognise the value of building long-term relationships with brands that align with their content, values, and audience. These lasting partnerships can offer consistent income, deeper brand integration, and a more authentic connection with your viewers. Long-term collaborations provide stability for both creators and brands, creating opportunities for mutual growth and success.

The Benefits of Long-Term Partnerships

Stability and Predictability

One-off deals can be lucrative, but they can also be sporadic. Long-term relationships provide more predictable income streams and a sense of stability. When you work with the same brand over time, you can plan your content calendar around these collaborations, reducing the stress of constantly seeking new sponsors. This consistency allows you to focus more on your creative work and audience growth rather than always needing to secure new deals.

Stronger Brand Affiliation

Over time, working with a brand repeatedly allows your audience to develop a deeper understanding of the brand and its values. The more frequently a brand is featured in your content, the more authentic and organic the partnership will appear. Viewers tend to trust creators who consistently work with the same brands because it indicates a genuine endorsement rather than a one-off promotional stunt. This consistency also helps to strengthen your personal brand by associating you with companies that share your values and resonate with your audience.

Increased Creative Control

With a long-term partnership, brands are often more willing to grant you the creative freedom to integrate their products into your content in a way that feels natural and fits seamlessly with your style. In contrast, one-off deals often come with more rigid guidelines and expectations. A brand that trusts you over time is more likely to give you the autonomy to craft compelling campaigns that align with your vision, allowing for a more authentic representation of their product.

Opportunities for Growth and Expansion

Long-term relationships provide opportunities for both you and the brand to grow together. As your audience and influence expand, so too can the scope of the partnership. Over time, brands may offer you more significant roles in their marketing campaigns, potentially elevating your status as a creator. Furthermore, a trusted relationship with a brand can open doors to new opportunities, including collaborations with other brands within the same network or industry.

How to Build Long-Term Relationships with Brands

Align with Brands That Share Your Values

When building long-term relationships with brands, it's essential to collaborate with companies whose products or services genuinely align with your values and your audience's interests. Brands that share your vision and ethos are more likely to respect and support you over the long term. For example, if you're a fitness-focused creator, partnering with a health-conscious brand will be a more natural fit than collaborating with a company whose products don't align with your content.

Working with brands that align with your values helps to maintain the authenticity of your content. Your audience is more likely to appreciate sponsored content when they see that it fits seamlessly into your overall narrative. Authenticity is crucial in ensuring that your viewers trust your recommendations and that your brand partnerships don't feel forced.

Deliver Consistent, High-Quality Content

To foster long-term relationships with brands, you need to consistently deliver content that meets or exceeds expectations. A reliable track record of high-quality, engaging content is a key factor in securing and retaining long-term sponsorships. Brands want to know that they can depend on you to maintain the same level of quality and consistency throughout your partnership.

Make sure that every piece of sponsored content you create is well-thought-out and aligns with the brand's goals. Keep in mind that your reputation as a creator is crucial to the success of these partnerships. Consistent quality content will not only satisfy your sponsors but will also keep your audience engaged and loyal.

Communicate Clearly and Professionally

Effective communication is at the heart of any successful partnership. Clear communication helps ensure that both you and the brand are on the same page in terms of expectations, deliverables, and goals. Be transparent about what you can offer and ensure that you understand the brand's objectives for the collaboration.

Throughout the relationship, keep the brand informed about the progress of your content, any feedback you've received from your audience, and how the campaign is performing. Regular updates foster trust and show that you are invested in the success of the partnership. Additionally, responding to feedback from the brand shows that you are open to collaboration and willing to make adjustments to improve results.

Be Transparent and Honest

Honesty is essential in building long-term, trusting relationships with brands. If something isn't working or if there's an issue with the partnership, be upfront and address it professionally. Transparency helps to prevent misunderstandings and ensures that both parties can work together to resolve any issues that arise.

Brands will appreciate your honesty and will be more inclined to continue working with you over time. Being open about what is working, what isn't, and how you plan to address any challenges will show that you are committed to the success of the collaboration and the long-term relationship.

Go Beyond Just Delivering the Deliverables

A long-term partnership isn't just about fulfilling contractual obligations; it's about building a relationship with the brand that goes beyond simply delivering sponsored content. Take the time to engage with the brand's team, understand their long-term objectives, and find ways to go above and beyond in your partnership.

For example, suggest new ideas for campaigns, offer additional value in the form of exclusive content, or provide creative input on upcoming product launches. By taking a proactive approach and offering new ideas, you demonstrate your commitment to the partnership and your willingness to invest in its success.

Focus on Mutual Growth

One of the main benefits of long-term partnerships is the opportunity for mutual growth. As your audience grows and your content evolves, look for ways to scale your partnerships with brands in a way that benefits both you and the sponsor. This could mean negotiating higher compensation or expanding the scope of your collaboration to include additional products or campaigns.

Long-term relationships allow both parties to evolve together. By focusing on mutual growth, you ensure that the partnership remains fresh, relevant, and beneficial to both sides.

Conclusion

Building long-term relationships with brands is a powerful strategy for YouTube creators who want to secure consistent, authentic, and successful sponsorships. These relationships offer stability, creative freedom, and opportunities for growth that one-off deals simply cannot provide. To establish lasting partnerships, it's crucial to work with brands that align with your values, deliver high-quality content, communicate clearly and professionally, and focus on mutual growth. By prioritising these aspects, you can build a strong foundation for long-term collaborations that benefit both you and your brand partners, leading to sustained success and lasting credibility in the industry.

Chapter-12

Stay Authentic: Only work with brands that align with your channel's ethos and audience interests to maintain trust and authenticity.

In the world of YouTube content creation, staying authentic is key to maintaining a strong, trusting relationship with your audience. As a creator, your audience follows you because they connect with your personality, values, and the content you produce. When it comes to brand partnerships, this authenticity is just as important. Collaborating with brands that align with your channel's ethos and audience interests not only helps preserve the trust you've built but also ensures that your content remains genuine and relevant.

The Importance of Authenticity in Brand Partnerships

Preserving Trust with Your Audience

Your audience is the backbone of your channel's success, and they value authenticity. When you promote a product or service that doesn't align with your usual content or values, it can create a sense of disconnection. Viewers may start to feel that you're simply trying to make money, rather than offering products or services that genuinely benefit them. This loss of trust can lead to disengagement, fewer views, and even unsubscribes.

By staying authentic and choosing to work with brands that align with your values, you maintain that trust and keep your audience engaged. When your viewers see that you only partner with brands that fit your ethos, they'll continue to trust your recommendations and will likely be more willing to purchase products you promote.

Creating Genuine Brand Integration

Authenticity in brand partnerships allows for more natural and seamless integration of sponsored content. When a product or service is a good fit for your channel, it becomes easier to talk about it in an organic way that feels true to your content. Whether it's a product that complements your niche or a service you already use and love, integrating it into your content feels more like a personal recommendation than a paid promotion.

This type of authentic integration is far more effective than forced or overly-scripted promotions. Brands are aware of this, and they seek creators who can deliver content that feels genuine. As a creator, choosing brands that align with your values and content style ensures that their message reaches your audience in a way that is both engaging and believable.

Building Long-Term Relationships with Brands

Working with brands that align with your ethos not only benefits your audience but can also lead to more sustainable, long-term partnerships. When you form authentic relationships with brands, they're more likely to return for future collaborations. These long-term deals are valuable because they provide steady income and allow for deeper integration of the brand into your content over time.

Additionally, when a brand sees that you genuinely believe in their product or service, they may be more willing to support your growth by offering better terms, higher compensation, or more opportunities. They understand the value of working with a creator who shares their values and mission, as it leads to more authentic and effective promotion of their product.

Avoiding the Pitfalls of Selling Out

There's a common fear among creators about "selling out" when it comes to brand partnerships. If you accept collaborations with brands that don't align with your channel's ethos, your audience may feel like you're sacrificing your integrity for money. This can damage your reputation and alienate the very people who support your channel.

Staying authentic allows you to avoid this pitfall. By only accepting partnerships that make sense for you and your audience, you demonstrate that you're not just in it for the financial gain. Instead, you're committed to providing value and ensuring that your content remains aligned with your values.

How to Stay Authentic in Brand Partnerships

Choose Brands that Align with Your Content and Audience

The most crucial step in staying authentic is selecting the right brands to work with. You should only collaborate with companies whose products or services complement your channel's niche, content, and audience interests. For instance, a beauty influencer might choose to partner with a skincare brand that aligns with their personal skincare routine and values, while a tech reviewer may collaborate with brands that produce innovative gadgets in line with their content.

Before committing to a partnership, evaluate whether the brand and its offerings make sense for your audience. Would your viewers be interested in the product? Is it something that you would use and recommend yourself? If the answer is yes, then it's more likely to be a good fit for your channel.

Be Transparent About Partnerships

Honesty is essential when it comes to sponsored content. Always disclose when a video is sponsored and ensure that your audience is aware of the nature of the partnership. Transparency is key to maintaining trust, and it shows your viewers that you're not trying to hide anything.

It's also important to be transparent in your content itself. If you're promoting a product, explain why you're promoting it and how it fits into your life or content. Don't just regurgitate a script; share your authentic thoughts and experiences with the product. Viewers can often tell when a creator is being genuine, and this transparency helps reinforce the authenticity of the promotion.

Limit the Number of Brand Deals

One of the risks of over-commercialisation is flooding your content with too many brand partnerships, which can detract from the authenticity of your channel. If your audience feels that you're prioritising sponsorships over your regular content, it could lead to viewer fatigue and decreased trust.

It's essential to strike a balance. Be selective about the number of brand deals you accept and ensure that the sponsored content doesn't overshadow your regular videos. Prioritise quality over quantity and only take on partnerships that feel like a natural fit for you and your audience.

Don't Be Afraid to Say No

Staying authentic means being comfortable with turning down brand deals that don't align with your content or values. As your channel grows, you'll likely be approached by numerous brands. While it's tempting to accept every offer that comes your way, not all of them will be right for you.

If a brand deal doesn't feel like a good fit, don't hesitate to turn it down. Saying no can help protect your integrity and prevent you from promoting products that may not resonate with your audience or align with your personal brand. By being selective, you maintain control over the partnerships you form and ensure that each collaboration is true to your values.

Stay True to Your Voice

Above all, staying authentic means staying true to your unique voice as a creator. Whether you're promoting a brand or not, your content should reflect your personality, interests, and perspective. Brands will appreciate the distinctiveness you bring to the table and will be more likely to offer long-term collaborations if they see that you have a strong, authentic presence.

When working with brands, continue to be yourself. Don't change your content style or voice to please a sponsor. If a brand wants to work with you, it's because of what makes you unique, so embrace that uniqueness and stay true to your identity.

Conclusion

Staying authentic in brand partnerships is crucial for maintaining the trust of your audience and ensuring the long-term success of your channel. By only working with brands that align with your ethos, content, and audience interests, you can create natural, seamless integrations that resonate with your viewers. Authenticity fosters trust, strengthens your relationships with brands, and helps you avoid the pitfalls of over-commercialisation. By being selective, transparent, and true to your values, you can successfully navigate brand partnerships while keeping your content genuine and maintaining the integrity of your channel.

Chapter-13

Create Sponsored Content Naturally: Seamlessly integrate sponsored content into your videos, making sure it aligns with your regular content style.

As YouTube creators, one of the most effective ways to monetise your channel is through sponsored content. However, integrating sponsored content into your videos without alienating your audience or disrupting your usual content style can be tricky. The key to successful sponsored content lies in making it feel natural—seamlessly blending the brand's message with your content so that it doesn't feel forced or out of place. When done correctly, sponsored content not only benefits the brand but also provides value to your audience, keeping them engaged and maintaining their trust.

Why Natural Integration Matters

Maintaining Audience Trust

Your audience follows you because they connect with your content, personality, and the authenticity you bring to the table. When sponsored content is integrated too abruptly or in a way that feels inauthentic, it can erode this trust. Viewers may start to feel that you're prioritising brand deals over their interests, leading to disengagement and potentially even unsubscribes. On the other hand, when you naturally integrate sponsored content into your videos, your audience feels like they're getting something of value without sacrificing the integrity of your channel.

Improved Viewer Experience

Seamlessly integrated sponsored content makes for a more pleasant and engaging viewing experience. Instead of interrupting the flow of your video, the content fits naturally within the narrative you're creating. It becomes just another part of the video, like any other topic you might cover. This approach keeps your viewers immersed in your content and prevents them from tuning out during the promotional segments.

Long-Term Sponsorship Opportunities

Brands are always looking for creators who can deliver results in an organic and engaging way. By mastering the art of natural content integration, you increase the chances of securing long-term sponsorships. Brands are more likely to return to creators who can incorporate their products in a subtle yet effective way, as this ensures that their message reaches the audience without disrupting the creator's authenticity.

How to Create Sponsored Content Naturally

Choose Relevant Brands

One of the most critical factors in making sponsored content feel natural is choosing brands that align with your channel's ethos and your audience's interests. When a product or service fits seamlessly into your regular content, it becomes much easier to incorporate it into your videos without it feeling like a forced advertisement. For instance, a tech reviewer should work with brands in the technology space, while a beauty influencer might choose skincare or makeup brands that resonate with their personal routine.

By partnering with brands that are relevant to your content, you ensure that your audience sees the promotion as something useful rather than a disruptive sales pitch. When your viewers recognise that you've chosen a product that fits naturally with your brand, they're more likely to trust your recommendation and take action.

Make the Integration Part of the Story

To make sponsored content feel natural, you should aim to weave the brand or product into the overall narrative of your video. This means discussing the product in a way that complements the topic at hand rather than making it feel like a standalone advertisement. For example, if you're creating a tutorial video, you can incorporate a product you're sponsored by as part of the process. For a fashion YouTuber, showcasing a brand's clothing line during a styling video creates a seamless connection between the brand and the content.

The key is to make the sponsorship feel like an integral part of the video rather than a disruption. By linking the brand to the storyline or theme of the video, you maintain the flow of the content and create a more authentic promotional experience.

Personalise the Promotion

A sponsored segment should feel like a genuine recommendation rather than a scripted advertisement. Personalising the promotion allows you to maintain your voice and style while still delivering the brand's message. Share your honest thoughts and experiences with the product. If it's something you already use or genuinely enjoy, your enthusiasm will come across as authentic. For instance, if you're sponsored by a fitness brand, showing how you incorporate their product into your workout routine will resonate more with your audience than simply reading off a script provided by the brand.

The more you can make the product feel like a natural extension of your content, the more engaging and authentic the sponsored segment will feel to your viewers. This helps your audience connect with the brand on a deeper level and increases the likelihood that they will act on your recommendation.

Avoid Overloading with Sponsored Content

One of the biggest mistakes creators can make when integrating sponsored content is overloading their videos with too many ads. If your audience feels like every video is filled with brand promotions, it can lead to viewer fatigue and decreased engagement. Instead, limit the frequency of sponsored segments to ensure that they don't dominate your content. Striking the right balance is key to maintaining the authenticity of your channel.

Integrating sponsored content naturally means that these segments should enhance the viewer experience, not detract from it. A few well-placed sponsorships can have a much greater impact than constantly bombarding your audience with ads.

Keep the Sponsored Content Aligned with Your Content Style

To maintain the natural feel of sponsored content, ensure that the way you present it aligns with your usual content style. Whether your videos are casual, educational, or highly produced, the way you incorporate sponsored content should match the tone and style of your regular videos. If you're known for your laid-back, conversational tone, keep the sponsored segment informal and true to that voice. On the other hand, if your videos are more structured or professional, incorporate the brand in a way that maintains that level of quality.

Consistency in the way you present sponsored content helps to preserve the flow of your videos and keeps the viewer experience cohesive. By matching your usual style, you ensure that the sponsorship doesn't feel out of place.

Engage with Your Audience During Sponsored Content

One of the best ways to make sponsored content feel natural is by engaging with your audience during these segments. Ask questions, encourage comments, and interact with your viewers about the product or service you're promoting. By making the sponsored content interactive, you create a more authentic and engaging experience that makes your viewers feel like they're a part of the conversation.

Additionally, creating a call-to-action that encourages viewers to share their experiences or thoughts on the product can further promote engagement. The more you engage with your audience, the less the sponsored segment will feel like an intrusion and more like a valuable part of the content.

Be Transparent About Sponsored Content

Transparency is essential when integrating sponsored content into your videos. Always disclose when a video or a segment within a video is sponsored. Not only is this a legal requirement, but it also maintains the trust of your audience. Your viewers appreciate honesty, and by being transparent about brand deals, you show that you respect your audience's intelligence and that you're committed to authenticity.

Clear and upfront disclosures also prevent any negative backlash, as your viewers won't feel like they're being tricked into watching a commercial. Whether you mention it at the beginning, middle, or end of the video, ensure that your audience knows when they're watching sponsored content.

Conclusion

Creating sponsored content naturally is about finding a balance between promoting a brand and maintaining the integrity of your content. When done right, it allows for smooth, engaging integration that benefits both the brand and the audience. By choosing relevant brands, personalising your promotions, aligning sponsored content with your regular content style, and engaging with your audience, you can create sponsored content that feels genuine and adds value to your videos. This authenticity strengthens your relationship with your viewers, keeps your content fresh and enjoyable, and ultimately enhances the success of your brand partnerships.

Chapter-14

Offer Exclusive Deals or Discounts: Provide value to your audience with special deals or discount codes from your sponsors, further enhancing the partnership.

One of the most effective ways to enhance your brand partnerships on YouTube is by offering exclusive deals or discount codes to your audience. When creators provide their viewers with special offers from sponsors, it not only strengthens the partnership but also adds tangible value to the relationship between the creator, the brand, and the audience. Exclusive deals and discounts can motivate your viewers to engage with the brand, make a purchase, and feel appreciated for their loyalty. However, it's important to integrate these offers in a way that feels authentic and genuinely beneficial to your viewers.

Why Exclusive Deals and Discounts Matter

Increase Engagement and Conversions

Offering exclusive discounts to your audience is a win-win situation. Your viewers get something of value, such as a limited-time offer or a special price, and the brand gets the exposure and potential sales. This creates an incentive for viewers to act quickly, leading to increased engagement and conversions. If your audience feels that they're getting a special deal that others don't have access to, they're more likely to follow through on their purchase.

Incorporating exclusive deals into your sponsored content also strengthens the partnership with the brand, as they see the direct benefits of collaborating with you. It shows that you can bring measurable results, which may open the door for future sponsorship opportunities.

Build Trust and Loyalty with Your Audience

By offering exclusive deals or discounts, you show your audience that you value them and their support. Instead of simply promoting a product for financial gain, you're giving your viewers something back, further deepening their connection with you. This sense of reciprocity can build long-term loyalty, as your audience feels more inclined to return to your channel, knowing that you consistently offer valuable content and deals.

When your audience sees that you're genuinely looking out for their interests—whether it's through sharing exclusive offers, discounts, or other perks—they're more likely to trust your recommendations and continue engaging with your content. This trust translates to higher viewer retention, better community engagement, and a stronger connection with the brands you partner with.

Enhance Brand Perception

For brands, having their products or services associated with exclusive deals helps enhance their perception among your audience. It gives the impression that the brand is offering something special or unique, and it creates an aura of exclusivity around the product. This can make the product more desirable, as limited-time offers often prompt customers to act quickly and secure a deal they might otherwise have overlooked.

Brands are often looking to strengthen their relationships with potential customers, and offering an exclusive deal through a trusted creator can be a very effective way to build that connection. For you as a creator, this enhances your credibility, as your audience knows you have access to exclusive offers that are not available elsewhere.

How to Effectively Offer Exclusive Deals and Discounts

Choose Deals That Align with Your Audience's Needs

One of the most important steps in offering exclusive deals is ensuring that the discount or offer aligns with your audience's interests. For example, a fitness influencer should partner with health and wellness brands that offer products your viewers are likely to use. Similarly, a beauty YouTuber should focus on skincare, makeup, or beauty tools that resonate with their followers.

Before offering a deal, take the time to understand the preferences of your audience. What products are they likely to be interested in? Are they already familiar with the brand you're collaborating with? By ensuring that the deal is relevant to your viewers, you increase the likelihood that they will use the discount code and share it with others.

Promote the Deal Creatively

To make your offer stand out, you need to promote it in a way that feels natural and engaging. A simple discount code or special offer can sometimes feel like an interruption if not done thoughtfully. Rather than just announcing the discount, try to incorporate it into your content seamlessly.

For example, if you're reviewing a product or doing a tutorial, you can mention the offer in a way that fits with the flow of the video. If you're hosting a Q&A or talking directly to your audience, casually mention the offer as something that benefits them. By weaving the promotion into your content, it doesn't feel like a forced advertisement and instead comes across as an added bonus for your viewers.

Additionally, showcasing how the product or service has worked for you, or how you genuinely use it, can increase the value of the discount offer. When viewers see you using the product and benefiting from it, they are more likely to take advantage of the deal themselves.

Create Urgency with Limited-Time Offers

Creating urgency is a powerful tool when promoting exclusive deals. Limiting the availability of the offer to a specific time frame or a certain number of purchases can encourage your audience to act quickly. Phrases like "limited-time offer" or "while stocks last" create a sense of urgency that can push viewers to make a purchase decision sooner rather than later.

Including a countdown in your video or a reminder about the offer's expiry date can also increase its effectiveness. The more urgent and exclusive the deal feels, the more likely your audience is to take action before the offer ends. This tactic works particularly well for products that have a strong appeal to your niche, as your audience will feel that they are getting access to something they can't get anywhere else.

Incorporate Multiple Touchpoints

To increase the impact of your exclusive offer, it's essential to promote it across multiple touchpoints. Don't just mention the deal once in the video and leave it at that. Encourage viewers to check out your social media, such as Instagram, Twitter, or Facebook, where you can share additional details or reminders about the deal.

Creating posts or stories that highlight the deal can help keep it at the forefront of your audience's mind. If you have an email newsletter or a Patreon account, use those platforms to send reminders and updates about the deal, ensuring your audience has multiple opportunities to access the offer. The more often your viewers see the deal, the more likely they are to take advantage of it.

Highlight the Value of the Deal

When promoting an exclusive offer, make sure to emphasise the value it brings to your audience. It's not just about the discount itself, but the overall value the audience will get by purchasing through the link or using the code. For example, you could mention that the discount will allow your viewers to try a high-quality product at a lower price, which is especially valuable for new customers who may be hesitant to make a purchase at full price.

By focusing on the benefits that your audience will experience, you make the offer more compelling and relevant. Viewers will appreciate knowing that the deal is not only exclusive but also offers them something they truly need or want.

Track Results and Share Success Stories

Finally, tracking the performance of your exclusive offers can help you measure the success of the campaign and optimise future deals. Monitor how many viewers are using the discount code and how much impact it has on conversions. If the deal is especially successful, share those results with your audience, which can further incentivise others to take advantage of future offers.

Sharing success stories, such as how many people have already used the deal or any feedback you've received from happy customers, can build credibility for the brand and encourage others to act quickly before the offer ends.

Conclusion

Offering exclusive deals and discounts is a great way to add value to your brand partnerships and enhance your relationship with your audience. By promoting special offers that are relevant, timely, and seamlessly integrated into your content, you can build stronger trust with your viewers, boost brand conversions, and create a mutually beneficial situation for both the brand and your audience. It's a powerful tool that not only rewards your viewers but also demonstrates your ability to drive results for the brands you partner with, leading to long-lasting and fruitful collaborations.

Chapter-15

Follow Legal and Ethical Guidelines: Ensure you follow all advertising regulations, such as clear disclosures and honest reviews, to maintain transparency and trust with your audience.

In the world of YouTube and online content creation, maintaining a solid relationship with your audience is crucial for long-term success. One of the key aspects that can significantly influence this relationship is the ethical and legal handling of sponsored content. As the influencer marketing industry continues to grow, legal regulations surrounding advertising and sponsored content have become more stringent. Creators must ensure they adhere to these regulations, as well as maintain ethical standards, to foster trust and transparency with their audience.

Adhering to legal and ethical guidelines not only protects you from potential legal issues but also shows your viewers that you are committed to integrity. This creates a positive environment for brand collaborations, ensuring that both your audience and sponsors benefit from your work. Below, we discuss why it's important to follow these guidelines and how you can do so effectively.

Why Following Legal and Ethical Guidelines Matters

Maintaining Transparency with Your Audience

Trust is the cornerstone of any successful content creator-audience relationship. Your viewers follow you because they believe in your authenticity and the value of your opinions. If you promote a product or service without full transparency, you risk alienating your audience. Viewers may feel misled, especially if they realise that your promotion was a paid sponsorship that was not clearly disclosed. This breach of trust can lead to decreased engagement, unsubscribes, and damage to your reputation.

By following legal guidelines, such as disclosing sponsored content clearly and honestly, you are showing your audience that you value their trust and are committed to being transparent. This transparency helps to maintain a strong and loyal following, which is vital for both the success of your channel and the long-term health of your brand partnerships.

Protecting Yourself Legally

In many countries, there are strict regulations surrounding advertising and sponsored content, and failing to comply with these laws can lead to fines, legal action, and damage to your reputation. In the UK, for instance, the Advertising Standards Authority (ASA) enforces rules to ensure that online advertisements, including sponsored content, are not misleading to the public. The UK's Committee of Advertising Practice (CAP) outlines specific requirements for disclosures, ensuring that content is clearly labelled as an advertisement.

Failing to disclose a paid promotion or sponsored content can result in penalties. For example, the ASA has the power to take down videos that violate advertising rules, and creators may face sanctions if they do not follow legal requirements. By understanding and following the advertising regulations, you protect yourself from potential legal consequences that could harm your channel's growth and future brand partnerships.

Ethical Responsibility as a Creator

As a content creator, you have an ethical responsibility to ensure that the products or services you promote align with your values and provide genuine value to your audience. This means being honest in your reviews and ensuring that the brands you collaborate with are reputable. Promoting subpar or misleading products may lead to viewer dissatisfaction and a loss of credibility.

Ethically speaking, it is also essential to disclose any material connection with a brand. When you are compensated for promoting a product or service, your audience deserves to know this. By following ethical guidelines and making honest endorsements, you demonstrate to your audience that your reviews and recommendations are unbiased and trustworthy.

Long-Term Success of Sponsored Content

When creators follow legal and ethical guidelines, they build lasting relationships with both their audience and sponsors. Brands prefer working with influencers who are transparent and adhere to advertising standards because it helps protect their reputation as well. Ethical conduct in advertising results in higher-quality partnerships and long-term collaborations.

Creators who prioritise ethical standards are more likely to secure future sponsorships, as they are viewed as trustworthy and professional. This can lead to higher-paying deals, better brand associations, and sustained growth for your channel.

Key Legal and Ethical Guidelines for Sponsored Content

Clear Disclosures

The most important aspect of following legal guidelines is ensuring that sponsored content is clearly disclosed. In the UK, the CAP and ASA require creators to disclose any paid partnerships or material connections with brands. This includes promotional videos, product placements, and affiliate links.

Disclosures should be prominent and unambiguous. YouTube offers tools that allow you to tag a video as 'sponsored' or 'contains paid promotion.' These labels should be visible from the beginning of the video to avoid any confusion. Additionally, it's important to mention the sponsorship in your video, verbally or through text, so your audience is immediately aware that the content is a promotion.

Honest Reviews and Authenticity

While it's important to comply with legal requirements, ethical considerations are equally vital. As a creator, you should provide an honest review of any product or service you endorse. If the product doesn't meet your expectations or you have concerns about its quality, it's your responsibility to share this with your audience.

Ethical conduct involves transparency in your opinions. If a brand wants you to review a product in a certain way or make unrealistic claims, you should feel empowered to reject these requests. Your audience relies on your genuine feedback, and maintaining authenticity in your reviews ensures that you don't lose their trust.

Avoiding Deceptive Practices

In addition to clear disclosures and honest reviews, creators must avoid deceptive advertising practices. For example, it's crucial not to exaggerate claims about a product's benefits or mislead your audience about its effectiveness. Providing false information not only damages your credibility but may also violate advertising laws.

For instance, a beauty influencer must avoid claiming that a product will 'cure' a skin condition if there is no scientific evidence to support such claims. By sticking to the facts and only promoting products you believe in, you ensure that your content is both ethical and legally compliant.

Clear Disclosure of Affiliate Links

If you're using affiliate links to promote products, it's essential to disclose this information clearly. Viewers need to know that you may earn a commission if they purchase through your link. This can be done by verbally or visually stating that the link is an affiliate link and that you may earn a commission if they use it.

The disclosure should be clear and easy to understand. Simply stating "this is an affiliate link" or "I may earn a commission from this purchase" ensures that your audience is fully informed and gives them the choice to support you in an ethical way.

Understanding the Rules Around Product Placement

Product placements, where a brand's product is featured in your content without direct promotion, are also subject to legal guidelines. These should be disclosed in the same way as sponsored content, as the audience needs to understand that the brand has paid for the inclusion of their product in the video. The disclosure should be clear and placed at the start of the video to avoid any potential confusion.

Compliance with Platform Guidelines

Beyond UK regulations, YouTube has its own community guidelines and policies that content creators must follow. These include restrictions on the types of sponsored content allowed on the platform. For instance, YouTube prohibits the promotion of certain types of products, including those that are illegal or violate its content policies.

Creators should familiarise themselves with both YouTube's advertising guidelines and the advertising standards in their country to ensure that their sponsored content complies with all applicable rules.

Conclusion

By following legal and ethical guidelines, YouTube creators ensure that they maintain transparency and trust with their audience. Disclosing sponsored content, providing honest reviews, and adhering to advertising regulations are fundamental to building long-term success as a creator. Not only does this safeguard you from potential legal issues, but it also strengthens your relationship with your audience, making your brand partnerships more effective and sustainable. In the fast-evolving landscape of digital marketing, staying true to these principles will allow you to navigate brand collaborations with integrity, ensuring a positive experience for both you and your viewers.

www.ingramcontent.com/pod-product-compliance
Lightning Source LLC
Chambersburg PA
CBHW071108240526
45469CB00006BD/2389